GUIDES TO RESPONSIBLE HUNTING
HUNTING ARMS

GUIDES TO RESPONSIBLE HUNTING

HUNTING ARMS

HUNTING SAFETY, LICENSING, AND RULES

PREPARING AND ENJOYING A MEAL YOU HUNTED

PREPARING FOR YOUR HUNTING TRIP

TRACKING AND HUNTING YOUR PREY

GUIDES TO RESPONSIBLE HUNTING
HUNTING ARMS

By Elizabeth Dee

MASON CREST

Mason Crest
450 Parkway Drive, Suite D
Broomall, Pennsylvania 19008
(866) MCP-BOOK (toll-free)
www.masoncrest.com

First printing
9 8 7 6 5 4 3 2 1

ISBN (hardback) 978-1-4222-4098-4
ISBN (series) 978-1-4222-4097-7
ISBN (ebook) 978-1-4222-7697-6

Library of Congress Cataloging-in-Publication Data
Names: Dee, Elizabeth, 1957- author.
Title: Hunting arms / Elizabeth Dee.
Description: Broomall, Pennsylvania : Mason Crest, [2019] | Series: Guides to responsible hunting | Includes index.
Identifiers: LCCN 2018006638 (print) | LCCN 2018002318 (ebook) | ISBN 9781422276976 (eBook) |
          ISBN 9781422240984 (hardback) | ISBN 9781422240977 (series) | ISBN 9781422276976 (ebook)
Subjects: LCSH: Hunting--Equipment and supplies. | Bow and arrow. | Hunting guns.
Classification: LCC SK273 (print) | LCC SK273 .D44 2019 (ebook) | DDC 639/.10284--dc23
LC record available at https://lccn.loc.gov/2018006638

Developed and Produced by National Highlights Inc.
Editor: Keri De Deo
Interior and cover design: Priceless Digital Media
Production: Michelle Luke

CONTENTS

KEY ICONS TO LOOK FOR:

Words to Understand: These words with their easy-to-understand definitions will increase the reader's understanding of the text while building vocabulary skills.

Sidebars: This boxed material within the main text allows readers to build knowledge, gain insights, explore possibilities, and broaden their perspectives by weaving together additional information to provide realistic and holistic perspectives.

Educational Videos: Readers can view videos by scanning our QR codes, providing them with additional educational content to supplement the text. Examples include news coverage, moments in history, speeches, iconic sports moments, and much more!

Text-Dependent Questions: These questions send the reader back to the text for more careful attention to the evidence presented there.

Research Projects: Readers are pointed toward areas of further inquiry connected to each chapter. Suggestions are provided for projects that encourage deeper research and analysis.

Series Glossary of Key Terms: This back-of-the book glossary contains terminology used throughout this series. Words found here increase the reader's ability to read and comprehend higher-level books and articles in this field.

 ## Words to Understand:

plinking: The practice of using small objects for target practice.

recoil: When a gun discharges a shot, the force will jerk the gun backward. This is also called a kick.

reloads: Homemade ammunition that should not be used by a young hunter.

scopes: These devices magnify objects to improve visibility for the shooter.

CHAPTER 1
HUNTING RIFLES AND AMMUNITION

Hunting can be the greatest outdoor adventure of a lifetime. Tracking and hunting game can provide a lot of fun and excitement for a young hunter. Plus, you will learn the valuable skills of responsibility, physical endurance, and keen observation. Young hunters know how to face problems with confidence as they learn how to provide food for themselves and others in the wild.

Hunting can be a way to enjoy the outdoors.

In the beginning, young hunters need plenty of guidance from their parents and hands-on practice to figure out how to handle their weapon safely. Learning to handle a gun correctly takes plenty of experience. Guns can be dangerous in the hands of someone who doesn't know what they are doing, but the responsible young hunter takes the time to learn how to handle a firearm safely.

CHOOSING A RIFLE

For the young hunter, a lightweight .22-caliber rifle makes an excellent choice for a starter gun. Such a small firearm can be transported or handled easily and doesn't have a strong kick or **recoil** when fired. The force of a larger rifle's recoil, such as a .30-30 rifle, can easily knock an adult of small stature backward onto the ground, especially if they don't expect the force of the kick. A .22 rifle doesn't have a hard kick or a loud report when fired, so a young hunter only needs minimum ear protection when using this type of gun.

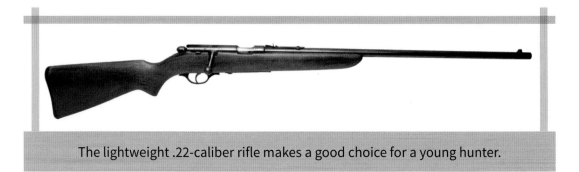

The lightweight .22-caliber rifle makes a good choice for a young hunter.

The versatile .22 rifle can be used for hunting small game, such as rabbits, birds, or squirrels, as well as for target practice or **plinking**. Plinking is target practice with small objects, such as a metal can. Hitting the can with a bullet makes the "plink" sound, and that's where plinking gets its name. Since target practice typically requires a lot of ammunition (or ammo for short), the .22 makes an excellent rifle choice because of the inexpensive price of the bullets for this gun. Remington, Winchester, and Browning rifles are well-made and reliable guns for young hunters.

A .410 is another great rifle for a young hunter, being lightweight, short in length, easy to load, and shoot. However, because of the smaller barrel size and narrower shooting range, this firearm requires greater accuracy when aiming at moving prey. However, a pump action on these hunting rifles allows for a quick second shot in case the first one misses! The .410 doesn't pack enough punch with recoil to knock anyone down which makes this rifle the right choice for even the youngest hunter.

Plinking is the sound a bullet makes when hitting a metal object like this tin can.

Loading a .22 is simple.

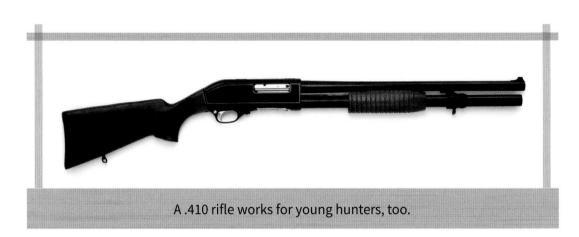

A .410 rifle works for young hunters, too.

Mossberg, Remington, and Browning manufacture some of the most popular .410 hunting rifles. Mossberg Mini rifles are designed primarily for small kids; with adjustable stocks that will expand as the child's height increases through the years, the gun grows with the young hunter.

TAKE CARE

Always remember that a hunting rifle is a weapon, and it can kill. Never shoot a firearm if you have the slightest doubt where or what that bullet will strike or if it will ricochet off a surface. Bullets can travel faster than the human eye can detect, so take care when shooting.

CHOOSING AMMUNITION AND SAFE DISPOSAL

Both .22 and .410 rifles commonly use three main types of bullets: 40 grain solid bullets, hollow point bullets, and a cheaper, 40 grain waxed bullet. Solid bullets have a rounded top, and hollow points have a hollowed-out area in the tip. Hollow point bullets expand on impact and make a larger hole in a target. Waxed bullets cause waxy buildup inside a gun, but they are still widely used because of the inexpensive price.

.410 waxed bullets are rather inexpensive

Ammunition not manufactured for use with a specific rifle should never be used with that firearm. The wrong ammo can lodge inside the rifle or cause it to misfire, severely hurting the hunter, or blasting apart the firearm, or both. Always take the time to read the instructions in the Owner's Manual or ask

A collection of African big game cartridges including (L to R) .400 Nitro Express, .500 Nitro Express, .600 Nitro Express, .700 Nitro Express and the 4 Bore with a dime to illustrate size.

a parent what ammo to use with a specific rifle. Also, read all of the printed material on the box of ammunition. When ready to load the rifle, check each bullet individually before loading it into the gun and make sure it is the correct caliber.

Reloads are the name given to bullets assembled at home by a hobbyist and not factory-made or purchased from a retail store. Inexperienced young hunters should not use this unstable type of ammo because of the danger involved. The performance of reloads can be unpredictable and can cause serious injury to a kid or teen as well as destroy a rifle if the bullet misfires.

If ammunition comes in contact with water or any other liquid, discard the bullets. Wet ammo can cause a rifle to jam or misfire. Never attempt to use a bullet if the casing looks dented. If a box of ammo is damaged during the packaging or shipping process, take it back to the store for a refund or dispose of it safely.

Any damaged or unused ammunition should be disposed of safely. Don't get rid of old ammo by throwing dented or otherwise damaged bullets in a trash can. Any ammo thrown in the trash poses a real threat because most garbage collected by a sanitation service uses a compactor. The force of the powerful crushing mechanism of a garbage truck's compactor can cause ammunition mixed with

The military uses special machines, like this one in Russia, to dispose of ammunition. (The international exhibition of armament, military equipment and ammunition RUSSIA ARMS EXPO (RAE-2013).)

trash to explode and perhaps injure a person. A typical bullet also contains lead, which creates a toxic load for the environment, so it should not go to a landfill.

Several options exist for old or damaged ammo disposal. In urban areas, contact the local police department and ask for assistance. A police officer may volunteer to assist in the disposal of the ammunition or give parents directions on how to get rid of it themselves. Another possibility involves dropping off the ammo at a waste facility that handles unsafe substances. They may agree to take the old ammo and dispose of it safely. Shooting ranges also offer safe options, such as conveniently located ammo disposal containers.

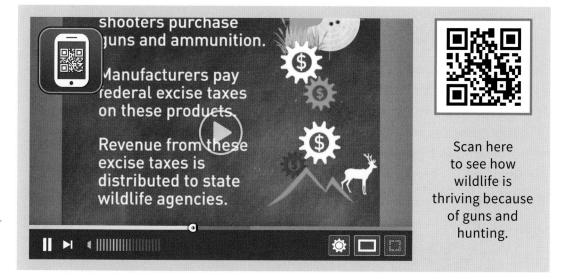

shooters purchase guns and ammunition.

Manufacturers pay federal excise taxes on these products.

Revenue from these excise taxes is distributed to state wildlife agencies.

Scan here to see how wildlife is thriving because of guns and hunting.

TREAT A LOADED GUN WITH RESPECT

RESPECT GUNS

Never play around with a gun. Don't let friends or acquaintances handle a rifle out of curiosity or point a firearm at friends or family as a joke, even if the gun doesn't contain bullets. When hunting with a rifle in the wild, make sure to only go out on hunts with parents or other responsible adults. Never take a firearm to school or a public place other than a shooting range.

A shooting range is a good place to practice shooting a gun.

Only load a rifle when hunting or shooting on a target range. When transporting a firearm, always unload the gun first because any jolts or bumps the vehicle encounters on the road may cause the gun to fire unexpectedly. Empty a rifle of bullets before storing it inside a camping tent or a home. While hunting or at home, never use a loaded rifle to poke or prod anyone. Don't be tempted to use a loaded gun to move an object, such as an obstructing tree limb, when out in the wild.

Always keep your gun barrel pointed down as you walk.

When walking through woods or fields with a rifle, keep the barrel pointed down toward the ground and never straight ahead. If there's a need to climb down a hill or cliff, always unload the rifle before starting the descent. Never climb trees or a deer stand with a loaded rifle. Young hunters should wait until they are sitting down in the deer stand and watching for the approach of prey before loading their weapon. Don't leap over obstacles, such as small boulders, streams, or stumps with a loaded gun. Jumping could cause inexperienced hunters to stumble and drop the rifle. Dropping a firearm can cause it to discharge, possibly injuring the shooter or another person.

USING EYE AND EAR PROTECTION

While shooting guns, beginner hunters should always wear hearing and eye protection. Guns make a lot of loud noise, and this can damage hearing over time. Wearing protective glasses while hunting in the wild will prevent eye injuries from such threats as insects, briars, and stray tree branches. These glasses also protect eyes in case of an accidental ricochet or a rifle casing that ejects too forcefully.

Eye and ear covers help protect your eyesight and hearing.

Some young hunters like to use yellow or orange tinted protective glasses to provide more contrast of targets and improve their shooting accuracy on a rifle range. Other colors can be utilized for different purposes as well, such as gray lenses that effectively block glare for use in bright sunlight or snow. For cloudy days with weak sunlight, amber lenses can help sharpen vision outdoors.

Wear protective glasses when cleaning or disassembling a rifle. These glasses will protect a person's eyes from toxic gun-cleaning fluid splashes or metal parts that could pop out of a disassembled gun and cause an eye or face injury. Choose wraparound styled glasses that don't leave an exposed gap between the glasses and skin. This style offers much more protection for the side of the face than other types.

STAY SAFE

Don't be careless with a gun because of the belief the safety device will keep the weapon from firing. Always handle a rifle carefully and keep fingers away from the trigger at all times to make sure the gun doesn't go off unexpectedly.

TIPS FOR GUN CLEANING

When disassembling a rifle for cleaning, study the Owner's Manual and follow all steps correctly. Don't remove more rifle parts than the Owner's Manual recommends. It may be too difficult to put back together again. Only clean the specific gun parts that the manual suggests. If a rifle will not reassemble after cleaning or a part becomes jammed, take the firearm to a professional gunsmith for inspection. Do not attempt to fire the rifle because this could result in personal injury or destruction of the weapon.

When cleaning a rifle for the first time, read the Owner's Manual for instructions and only use substances recommended by the manufacturer. Using other chemicals may damage the "bluing" or finish of the metal parts or destroy the finish of the stock. Wooden stocks have been factory varnished,

Always follow manufacturing instructions for cleaning a gun.

JEREMY WAITS, HUNTER – LESSONS FROM AN OLD GUN

 When Jeremy was a teenager, he received a shotgun that belonged to his great-grandfather. The gun is a .410 lever action shotgun purchased approximately in the late 1930's. Jeremy took excellent care of the shotgun through the years, lubricating the moving or "action parts" with gun oil on a regular basis. He also oiled the wooden stock to protect the finish. Jeremy kept the shotgun inside a case so it wouldn't become scratched from everyday handling. The result is the gun still looks new and works great even though it is approximately 80 years old.

The shotgun has a solid wood stock instead of the synthetic stocks used on new guns. Jeremy said that when he cleans the shotgun, he doesn't take it apart for every cleaning, but he is diligent to make sure the whole gun is cleaned well, especially if it got wet while out hunting.

Jeremy has used this old shotgun on many hunts and made his first kill with this weapon. He says he always treated the .410 with the utmost respect and not like it was a toy. He is proud of the fact he never had any accidents or issues while hunting because he obeyed the rules.

and the wood should be cleaned with products sold for this purpose. Be careful not to damage synthetic or plastic gun stocks with strong solvents or cleaning fluids that can soften and ruin the plastic. After cleaning a hunting rifle, make sure to wipe away layers of oil or any lubricant before loading the gun with bullets.

A gun can last many generations if treated properly.

Jeremy takes his .410 on many hunting adventures.

Never attempt to clean a gun before emptying out all of the ammunition and be careful not to touch the rifle's trigger when unloading it for cleaning. After cleaning a gun, store all bullets in a secure place away from anyone who should not have access to the ammunition. Store the rifle separately from the bullets.

Thoroughly cleaning a rifle after each use helps prevent many problems. Keeping a gun clean and dry will ensure reliability when it comes to firing and will extend the life of a firearm. When fired, tiny flakes of metal, gunpowder, and other substances coat the inside of a rifle's barrel. If the buildup continues without cleaning, the gun will eventually jam or fail to operate. Some inexpensive brands of ammunition cause waxy residue to form and the gun should be cleaned more frequently. When storing a firearm for an extended period between hunting seasons, remember to clean it well before use. Stored firearms can form a lot of rust on the inside of the gun, especially in a humid climate.

DID YOU KNOW?

Annie Oakley, a famous exhibition shooter of the Wild West, stated that her favorite gun to use for her amazing tricks was a .22 caliber rifle. Annie became famous as a teenager in 1885 for blasting playing cards in half and shooting cigarettes out of the mouths of volunteers. She would also toss a coin into the air and shoot a hole through it before it touched the ground.

1880's poster for Buffalo Bill's Wild West show, advertising "Miss Annie Oakley, the peerless lady wing-shot."

RIFLE SCOPES AND RECOIL PADS

Rifle scopes or sights magnify objects and make it easier for the young hunter to aim and hit targets at a distance. Hunters who have less than perfect vision can use a scope to help improve their shooting accuracy. However, there are drawbacks to putting a scope on a small gun. Young hunters use small rifles for short range shooting, and the wrong scope can make objects in close range appear fuzzy and indistinct. If a rabbit suddenly leaps into a hunter's path and they are peering through a long-range rifle scope, the rabbit will look like a moving blur, and the young hunter won't be able to take aim and shoot.

Guns with scopes are popular hunting tools.

Using a variable-magnification rifle scope can help with this problem. These adjustable scopes bring the objects in close range into sharper focus as well as provide clarity for far away targets. This adjustability provides a wider range of clear viewing. For a young hunter's rifle, choose a lightweight scope. It's not a good idea to put a big scope on a small firearm because the heavy weight of the scope will make the rifle unwieldy and slower to manipulate.

Attaching a scope to a small hunting rifle usually doesn't require a gunsmith to do the job. However, don't sloppily attach a scope to a rifle and expect it to work properly. Scopes or sights must be firmly attached to function properly and improve the hunter's aim.

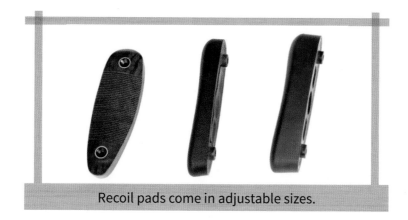

Recoil pads come in adjustable sizes.

Using recoil pads can help with the sharp kick of a rifle, especially for beginners of smaller stature. Recoil pads absorb the shock of a gun's kick that can cause soreness or bruising of the shoulder over time. Materials such as foam or rubber encase the butt of a firearm to protect the young hunter's shoulder and upper arm muscles. A recoil pad will also help a smaller kid keep a firmer hold on the rifle by providing friction against their clothing, such as a hunting jacket. The friction prevents the gun from sliding downward when held at shoulder height.

TEXT-DEPENDENT QUESTIONS:

1. What should you do first when cleaning a rifle?

2. When walking through the woods with a rifle, do you point the barrel straight ahead?

3. What can you do to minimize the kick of a rifle?

RESEARCH PROJECT:

Research the scientific process behind the process of how a gun fires a bullet. What do you think is the future of guns and how will they be used fifty years from now? Write a two-page report on your findings and present it to your class.

Try building a Gauss rifle using magnets and ball bearings. Measure how far a Gauss rifle will launch a ball bearing.

Words to Understand:

bolt-action: This type of firearm uses a handle to manually open the barrel for ejecting spent casings and loading ammunition.

breech-loading: A firearm loaded from the rear end of the barrel.

choke: A choked barrel of a gun is the inside dimensions of the barrel reduced in size at the firing end. A choke is an attachable device that narrows a shotgun's barrel.

lever-action: This gun uses a lever located near the trigger guard to load bullets for shooting.

pump-action: A firearm that uses the action of a forward sliding component, called a forend, to eject a shotgun shell casing after firing. The forend is manually slid forward and backward in a quick action and out pops the empty shell casing.

semi-automatic: With no need to reload after each shot, these types of firearms can shoot one shotgun shell after another.

tang safety: A sliding safety button that keeps a gun from firing.

CHAPTER 2
SHOTGUNS

THE SHOTGUN

Shotguns, sometimes called scatterguns, are smoothbore firearms and come in many sizes. Smoothbore means the inside of the barrel does not have the rifling, or spiraling grooves, carved into the metal. Shotguns are fired from the shoulder like rifles and many young hunters like to use these guns for short-range shooting.

Scatterguns come in different sizes.

For ammunition, a shotgun uses small shot, which consists of many small pellets of lead or other metal packed tightly into a plastic and metal cartridge. When using many pellets instead of one single bullet, the shot will scatter or spread out, and the chance of hitting the intended target is much greater.

The scattering action will help a young hunter to hit fast-moving targets, such as a flock of small birds flying past.

A shotgun uses small shot packed tightly into a plastic and metal cartridge.

HISTORY OF THE SHOTGUN

When choosing a shotgun as your weapon of choice, you are selecting a historical weapon. The shotgun has its roots deep in the past, evolving from firearms used in the 18th century. The musket is one ancestor of the shotgun, and a soldier that used a musket was called a musketeer. Another grandfather of the modern-day shotgun is the blunderbuss. This weapon had a short barrel used for short-range shooting, usually by soldiers that engaged in close quarters combat.

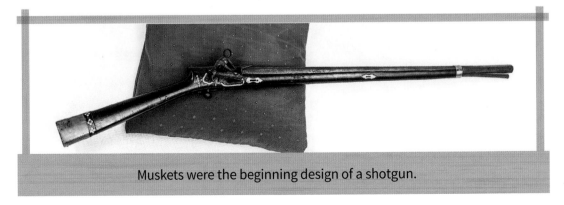

Muskets were the beginning design of a shotgun.

A blunderbuss was used on stage coaches and to fight wars.

As the design of the shotgun progressed through the years, **breech-loading** types were developed. Loading a gun from the rear was believed to be a quicker way of loading ammunition as opposed to loading the gun from the front.

In the American Old West, use of the shotgun became very popular because it requires less skill and accuracy to hit a target than a rifle or pistol. Stagecoach drivers carrying mail or passengers rode with a guard armed with a shotgun for protection against fast-moving robbers on horseback. The term 'riding shotgun' comes from this era of history.

Stagecoaches like this one in Jackson Hole, Wyoming often needed armed guards to help keep passengers and cargo safe.

SHOOTING INTO WATER

Shooting at fish or snakes in the water may be lots of fun but don't do it. There could be hard objects, such as large stones, hidden under the water that could cause gunshot to ricochet and cause a serious accident.

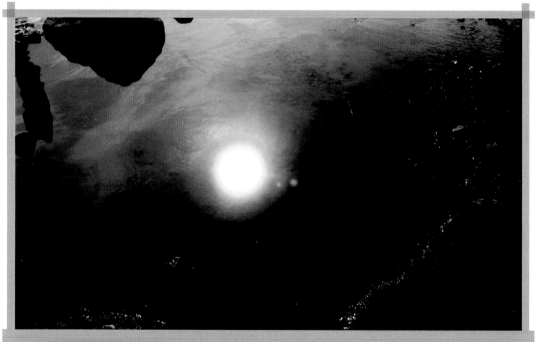

You never know what's beneath the surface of the water, so do not shoot into the water.

If you are a beginner, always handle a shotgun in the presence of a responsible adult that can supervise. When out in nature, never lean a shotgun against a tree or other object. The gun could fall over, hit the ground, and discharge. Don't pick up other people's guns and handle them for any reason. It might be loaded, and you would not know. Beginning hunters should only handle a firearm they have experience with and only in the presence of an adult.

TYPES OF SHOTGUNS

Shotguns come in many sizes and variations for different uses. For the young hunter, a smaller, lighter weight shotgun would be the best choice. A smaller gun is handled easier by a beginning hunter just learning to shoot and handle a firearm. A lighter weapon is also much easier to carry on long hikes through the woods or fields when hunting.

A 10-gauge, 12-gauge, or 16-gauge shotgun makes a good starter shotgun for a young hunter just learning how to load a gun and practice firing. Shooting at stationary targets helps a beginner develop aim and a steady hand when holding a gun. With plenty of target practice, they can also work out how to pull the trigger of their shotgun in a smooth manner and overcome any jerky, awkward movements. Every young hunter should develop smoothness in handling a gun before participating in a hunt for wild game.

Pick a shotgun that's the right size for you and will be easy to carry.

Get lots of practice shooting at
a target before hunting.

20-gauge shotguns do not have as much of a forceful kick or recoil if you use low-recoil ammunition, which is essential for a small hunter. Don't give up shooting if you experience pain from recoil. Try changing ammunition instead.

The size of the shotgun must fit the size of the hunter using it. Don't use a shotgun that's too long or too heavy because it will be hard to carry and shoot straight. A gun that's too big can cause a young hunter to have an accident. A shotgun that's an awkward size can interfere with accuracy when shooting and slow down response time when hunting. A slow response time means a lot fewer hunting trophies.

Pump-action shotguns, with a forend that slides back and forth, will make shooting easy for a younger hunter. Pump-action guns are lighter in weight and considered safer than the average gun when it comes to loading them with ammo. **Lever-action** and **bolt-action** shotguns are somewhat harder to use and make a better gun for an older hunter who has more experience and more strength in their hands to handle the lever or bolt.

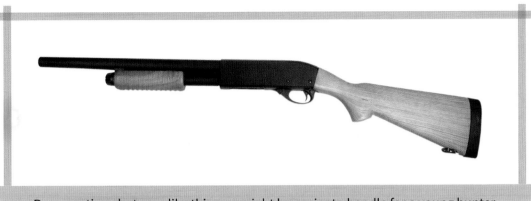

Pump-action shotguns like this one might be easier to handle for a young hunter.

Lever-action shotguns like this one might be best for a more experienced hunter.

BEST SHOTGUNS FOR YOUNG HUNTERS

The Remington 870 Express Compact Jr. shotgun is a safe gun for even the smallest of hunters. These pump-action shotguns have adjustable stocks that will lengthen as the young hunter grows in height.

Winchester SXP Field Compact is another pump-action shotgun suitable for the younger hunter. This gun is lightweight, easy to use, and very compact.

Mossberg 500 Super Bantam is another reliable gun for the small hunter. A pump-action shotgun, the Mossberg makes a good choice for left-handed kids because of the location of the **tang safety.**

A pump-action shotgun might be the best gun for young hunters. Try out several before buying one.

AMMO USED FOR SHOTGUNS

When shotguns fire, the many pellets that make up the shot spread out in a wide pattern. This spreading action makes it easier to hit the target, but the multiple pellets do not have the same powerful impact of a single bullet. However, a shotgun using pellets for ammo makes a good choice for hunting

Keep your eyes on your dog at all times when hunting so your dog is not in the line of fire.

birds and other small animals for food. Using pellets makes it easier to hit a target like a fast-moving bird or small animal, and the small pieces of shot don't tear the meat to pieces and make it unfit for eating.

HUNTING WITH DOGS

When hunting with dogs, be sure to keep track of their location at all times. Never fire blindly at movement in the bushes or long grass because it could be the dog exploring and sniffing around for birds or rabbits. The same rule applies if hunting with others. Make sure each hunter is in plain sight of the others at all times. Otherwise, someone could get shot by accident.

Before shooting at a target, animal, or bird, be sure the dogs or other hunters are not close enough to be hit with the spread of shot from a shotgun. If an animal, such as a rabbit, crosses the path between a hunter and their dog or hunting companion, do not shoot! The gunshot may hit the prey, but it may also hit the dog or another hunter.

Shotgun barrels are very hot to the touch after firing and can easily burn your fingers. Be careful how you handle the gun until it cools down. Pick up empty shells to dispose of later. Don't leave any litter in the wild.

Responsible hunters pick up their empty shells.

SHOTGUNS ARE GREAT FOR TARGET SHOOTING

Double-barreled shotguns are a favorite gun to use in target shooting, such as skeet shooting. Skeet shooting uses a clay disk, called a pigeon, thrown into the air by a machine designed to imitate a bird's flight. Use skeet practice to help develop the quick reflexes needed to shoot down flying birds. Skeet shooting helps a young hunter develop aim and better accuracy with the shotgun.

Skeet shooting is one way to keep your shooting skills sharp.

Experiment with **chokes** and different types of shot to find out what works best for you. Remember, when aiming at flying birds, there's rarely a chance for a second shot because they are so fast. A beginner hunter should practice skeet shooting as much as possible if they wish to become a successful bird hunter.

DOUBLE-BARRELED SHOTGUNS

Double-barreled shotguns have two barrels, and these guns are breech-loaded with ammunition. A mechanical catch is used to disengage the barrel, and the gun pops open where the hunter inserts the shotgun shells. Opening a gun this way is called a break open action. When walking through woods or fields with a breech-loaded firearm, the hunter usually breaks the gun open and carries it over their arm as a safety measure. When held in the break open position, the gun can't fire.

Double-barreled shotguns are suitable for older, more experienced hunters because the weapon can be heavy to carry and has a much harder recoil when fired than a single barrel. The heavy recoil could knock down a small hunter. With a double discharge, these guns have a lot of firepower, meaning you should use these shotguns for hunting larger game, such as deer.

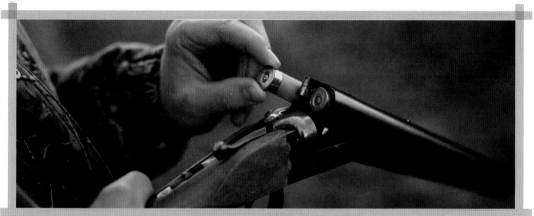

Double-barreled shotguns are appropriate for more experienced hunters when hunting large game.

A HUNTING STORY BY JEREMY WAITS, HUNTER

Jeremy, his twin brother, and his father joined a hunting club when he was twelve. Both boys had gotten shotguns for Christmas. Dad and both boys spent the following spring and summer months scouting for signs of deer and building a deer stand by a creek in the spot of the most deer activity. Jeremy continued to practice with his 12-gauge shotgun for the rest of the summer, improving his aim. When autumn rolled around, he was ready for his first hunt. However, he didn't have any luck that year.

The next year was different. Jeremy was sitting in the deer stand, which he described as "just two pieces of plywood nailed between two trees," when three does walked up to the creek to drink water. Jeremy quickly fired his shotgun at the trio, and the deer ran away. He thought he had missed the mark. With his father, Jeremy ran down to the creek and there lay his first kill!

Hunting can be an excellent family activity.

USING CHOKES WITH A SHOTGUN

Using a choke on a shotgun improves a beginner hunter's accuracy when firing because it narrows the inside of the barrel and creates a smaller space for the pellets to pass out of the barrel. Some shotguns are manufactured with chokes, and others have machined threads added so a hunter can screw in a choke whenever needed.

Chokes are very useful when hunting turkeys because the small head of the bird is so hard to hit. Wild turkeys are usually shot in the head or neck to preserve the body for eating. Using too much choke will narrow the spray range of the shot and make it extra hard to hit the turkey's head, while too little choke can allow the pellets to scatter and destroy the edible meat of the bird. Using a particular type of choke used just for turkey hunting can solve these problems.

When hunting for birds that fly in flocks, use a wide choke to help in bringing down multiple flying birds. When using a wide choke, the young hunter doesn't have to be very close to the flock of birds to make a kill.

DID YOU KNOW?

No matter who you are it pays to be careful with a gun! Even famous people in the past have shot themselves accidentally with a firearm.

Al Capone, a notorious American gangster during the Prohibition, accidentally shot himself twice in his lifetime. Capone was the real-life Scarface and believed to be responsible for the St. Valentine's Day Massacre.

Even though Capone surrounded himself with bodyguards, he always carried a gun hidden in his golf bag with his clubs when he played golf. On that fateful day, Capone had just finished a game and picked up his golf bag from the ground. His hidden gun fired and hit him in the foot.

Eye witnesses believed that the movement of the golf clubs inside the bag made the gun fire. Capone was taken to the nearest hospital, was treated, and recovered. However, he shot himself for the second time in the groin as he was exiting a car, with a gun hidden on his person. Again, Capone survived the accident.

Peter Fonda, a well-known actor, and son of famous movie star Henry Fonda, was playing with a revolver when he was eleven years old and accidentally shot himself in the chest area, narrowly missing his heart. Peter barely survived the incident, and it took months for him to recover fully.

Cowboy Shotgunning Equipment and Loading - Cowboy Action Shooting. The National Shooting Sports Foundation. YouTube, 2012.

Choke tubes help with shooting accuracy.

WHY DO HUNTERS WEAR THAT BRIGHT ORANGE COLOR?

Most state hunting laws require all hunters to wear the bright orange color while out deer hunting. The color is worn for safety reasons. That super-bright color goes by the name of blaze orange or hunter orange, and scientists say a deer's eyes can't detect it because they are color blind. However, a fellow hunter can see the color quite easily and from a long distance. That's why blaze orange was chosen for hunters. Blaze orange stands out brightly against the colors of nature and makes the young hunter wearing that color very visible to other hunters in the area.

The bright orange color reduces the possibility of an accidental shooting when hunting on public land. It also helps emergency techs to locate your position if you are hurt on a hunt and have called for help on a cell phone. You don't want to be mistaken for a deer or other animal while hunting in the woods, so always wear plenty of blaze orange clothing!

TEXT-DEPENDENT QUESTIONS:

1. How does skeet target practice prepare a young hunter for shooting birds in the wild?

2. What is another name for a shotgun?

3. What does the term 'riding shotgun' refer to in a historical context?

RESEARCH PROJECT:

Compare the way ammunition for a rifle works with that of shotgun ammo. How do they work differently? What are the pros and cons of each? Get opinions from three adult hunters and compare them. Write down your thoughts on which ammunitions would work the best in different situations and with different types of wild game. Discuss your thoughts with the three adult hunters and write down their responses. How did their opinions differ from yours?

 Words to Understand:

draw weight: The amount of physical strength it takes for an archer to pull back a bowstring.

fletching: The term for the feathered trim on the end of the arrow that stabilizes it in flight.

limbs: These parts are made of flexible fiberglass and attach at the top and the bottom of a compound bow.

nock point: The place on a bow string where to "nock" or locate an arrow before taking aim and shooting.

riser: This is the middle part where hands hold onto the bow.

quiver: This container usually straps to the hunter's back and holds extra arrows.

THE BOW AND ARROW

There are four main types of bows used in game hunting. These include the longbow, the recurve bow, the compound bow, and the crossbow. If you are under the age of nine, you should start practicing with a bow with a draw weight of only ten pounds, so you won't have soreness or muscle pain after shooting.

Bowhunting can be a rewarding sport.

Small hunters should begin the sport with target practice only and use a smaller weapon, such as a recurve bow. When young hunters are older and have grown tall enough to handle a larger draw weight bow, they can use a bigger weapon and hunt for wild game. Lots of target practice, in the beginning, will provide valuable experience and will help the beginning hunter learn all about safety rules and the methods for using a hunting bow. Later, the young hunter can use these skills in the woods or fields for wild game.

YOU MUST HAVE THE RIGHT SIZED EQUIPMENT

When learning how to hunt with a bow, it's important for a beginning hunter to have the right sized equipment for their height and level of strength. A hunter should always pick the bow that feels the best in their hands and isn't too heavy.

If a bow has too much draw weight or is too long, the weapon will be awkward to use and a beginner will have a lot of trouble handling the weapon. Their bow shots will be clumsy and will usually miss the mark. A wrong sized weapon can cause a beginning hunter to feel a lot of frustration and disappointment. Eventually, this situation could cause a beginner to give up completely because they believe they lack the talent to shoot well.

To be proficient in bowhunting, it takes lots of target practice.

JEREMY WEIGHS IN ON HUNTING WITH BOWS

If you are having trouble handling a bow well, don't give up! Jeremy says a bow and arrow is harder to handle than a gun and can make hunting more difficult for the beginner. Bow hunting requires a lot more practice to overcome the special challenges of the weapon than a rifle or shotgun. He recommends to keep practicing your stance and shooting arrows as much as possible, and eventually you will become a successful bow hunter.

Jeremy says the main fact a beginning hunter needs to understand is how to estimate the distance between a deer and the hunter. The further an arrow travels in flight, the more it will drop to the ground. This drop needs to be calculated by the hunter in order for the arrow to strike the deer. Some bows have built-in devices called pins or sights that will help a hunter calculate the drop.

THE HUNTING BOW THROUGHOUT HISTORY

This ancient rock drawing found in Uzbekistan depicts a hunter with a bow and arrow.

This is a compound bow.

Crossbows - This is another bow used since ancient times. However, some provinces in Canada as well as some states in America have outlawed the crossbow for hunting or limited its use only for the disabled. Crossbows are held horizontally and use a crank to draw back the bowstring. A trigger is pulled to fire the crossbow when ready. Known for their short ranges when shooting, these bows are typically used for target practice and shooting game at close range. The arrows used by a crossbow are called bolts, and they are much shorter in length than a regular arrow.

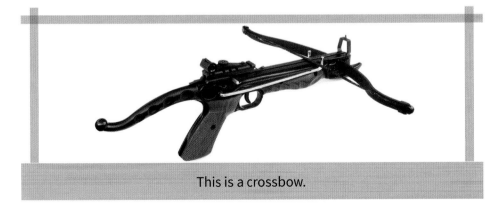

This is a crossbow.

TYPES OF ARROWS

The shaft of an arrow can be made of many substances, such as aluminum, fiberglass, or wood. An arrow should always be equal in strength to the bow to prevent an arrow from breaking. Don't use damaged arrows, such as ones that are cracked or splintered, and don't stand too close to another person if you suspect they are shooting a bow with a less than perfect arrow. A damaged arrow will not stay on course and can cause a serious accident to a bystander. The **fletching** should also be in good shape for an arrow to fly straight.

For hunting small game, use steel point or blunt point arrowheads. The blunt points are also used for target practice. Blunt point arrowheads are made out of a softer material such as plastic or rubber which is a better arrowhead for shooting at a target range.

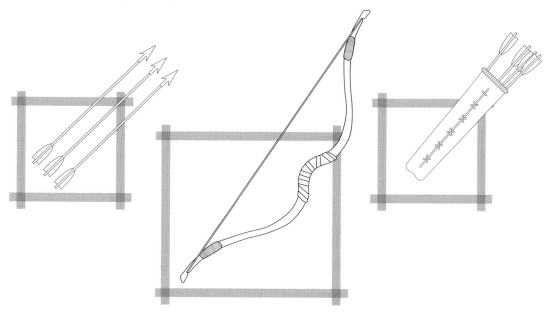

THE DANGEROUS BROADHEADS

The best arrow tip for hunting bigger game like deer, elk, or moose is the broadhead. Broadhead arrow tips are constructed with a steel center and have very sharp steel blades like wings that stand out from the center rod.

These arrowheads are used exclusively for large game. Handle these arrow tips carefully. The broadhead arrow tip is specifically designed to slice into flesh quickly and cut through arteries and veins efficiently to make the kill as swift as possible. When hunting a big animal, the young hunter needs to make the kill as fast as possible because a large wounded animal can be dangerous.

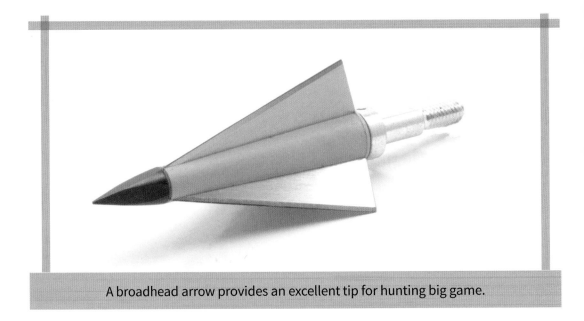

A broadhead arrow provides an excellent tip for hunting big game.

When carrying arrows in a **quiver** on a hunt, always make sure the sharp ends of arrows are completely covered. A teen hunter should be extra careful when carrying broadheads because they are razor-sharp and can cause a serious injury very easily. You don't want to slice open your hand while on a hunt far away from the nearest hospital.

The beginner hunter should never bow hunt with a broadhead. They are too dangerous for someone with little experience with these arrowheads. Only older hunters with a lot of experience should use these types of arrow tips.

When attaching a broadhead onto an arrow, be sure to use a wrench designed for this purpose. The wrench will cover the sharp edges of the broadhead and prevent an injury. Use specially-made hard plastic cases or individual safety covers to store and transport these deadly arrowheads instead of a quiver.

Encasing the extra sharp blades will prevent accidents, such as cutting fingers on the sharp edges. Keep broadheads in safety covers while traveling or transporting hunting equipment in vehicles because they can jab through most any material and stab the hunter.

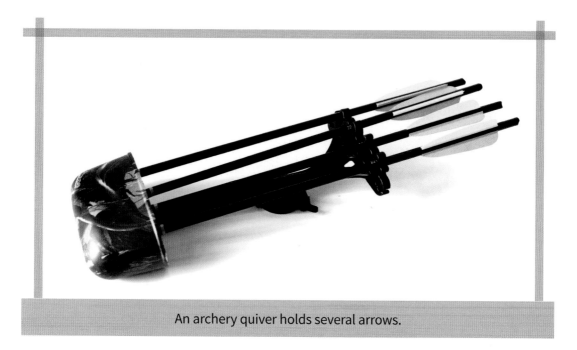

An archery quiver holds several arrows.

PRECAUTIONS BEFORE SHOOTING

Before bow shooting of any kind, carefully inspect all of your equipment to be used during the session. Discard in a safe manner arrows that show any sign of damage or warpage. Don't use such arrows under any circumstances. Damaged arrows can shatter during shooting and cause damage to the bow and the young hunter. Never use the wrong arrow for your bow. Shooting a weaker arrow from a stronger bow will destroy the arrow.

Flexing an arrow with both hands is a good way to test it before shooting. Pay close attention to the arrow as you flex it. If it makes a cracking sound or splinters, do not use it. Replace the damaged arrow with a good one, nock it, take aim, and shoot!

Examine all of your equipment
before shooting any arrow.

WEAR THE PROPER GEAR

When hunting with a bow, special protective equipment is needed to keep the archer safe and free from injury. Bowstrings can whip forward with a considerable force which can injure skin or bruise the muscles underneath. When drawing a bow, keep the string away from the face, eyes, and hair.

To protect their fingers from bowstring injuries, archers will need to wear three-fingered thick gloves during target practice or while hunting. Another device that can protect the fingers is a mechanical release with a built-in trigger. The release snaps onto the bowstring, and when pulled into firing position, the mechanical release will hold the bowstring in place until ready to be fired. Pressing the trigger will fire the arrow.

Thick, three-fingered gloves will protect your fingers from injury.

Wearing an armguard protects the inner part of the hunter's forearm while shooting an arrow. When the powerful bowstring is released, the armguard acts as a shield to keep the string from damaging the arm or striking against clothing and throwing the arrow dangerously off course. In the event an arrow snaps in two or splinters into pieces during a shoot, the armguard will protect the young hunter's arm from the flying pieces.

One piece of protective equipment that might be useful is an armguard.

JEWELRY, CLOTHING, AND HAIR

Before firing a hunting bow, be sure to remove anything that might be in the path of the bowstring. Long necklaces, earrings, scarves, earphone cords, and even long hair should be kept safely out of the way of the bowstring to avoid a painful accident. Be careful when wearing heavy or very loose clothing so that the bowstring doesn't catch on the cloth.

SHOOTING THE ARROW

When shooting an arrow, it's important to place the arrow on the same spot on the bowstring to ensure the accuracy of the shot. The official name for this spot is called the **nock**. If you place the arrow too high or too low on the bowstring, this will affect the angle of the shot, and you won't hit the target.

When preparing to shoot a hunting bow, you should stand straight and evenly balanced on both feet. Don't spread your feet too far apart or keep them too close together. Your feet should be approximately in a parallel line with your shoulders. If wearing heavy clothing, such as a hunting jacket or vest with big pockets that protrude outward, make sure the cloth and the pocket flaps are kept out of the way of the bowstring. Don't let the action of the bowstring catch on your shoulder and throw off your shot.

A hunting bow can be just as deadly as a gun. Only shoot an arrow when you are absolutely sure it will hit nothing but the target. Don't shoot wildly, straight upward, or into the distance further than can be seen with the human eye. Shooting into the unknown can injure or kill other people or pets. Arrows shot straight upward into the air can kill on the descending path. Be extra careful when bow hunting with a dog as well, because they can suddenly dart in front of a hunter right as they attempt to shoot an arrow.

A young hunter should only hold an arrow in a nocked position when directly approaching prey, such as a deer spotted in the woods. Never nock an arrow while walking behind another person or a hunting dog while in the outdoors, even if a deer or rabbit is expected to appear suddenly.

Don't climb up into a hunting stand with a bow and quiver of arrows. Tie a hauling line to the equipment instead and draw up the bow and quiver safely. Falling from a tree with razor-sharp arrow tips could cause a fatal injury, so it's best to haul them up with a line.

While hunting in the woods, arrows can be easily knocked off course after firing. Hitting a hard surface or a tree branch can cause an arrow to bounce, veer off course, and cause an accident, so this is another reason not to shoot anywhere near another hunter.

Proper Release and Bow Hand Placement for Archery.

THE ARCHER'S STANCE

For the best results in archery or hunting, assuming correct posture while shooting the bow is important. Good posture will affect the accuracy of the aim. Stand up as straight as possible with your neck held erect. Don't slump forward in the slightest. Turn your head toward the target without twisting the torso as you aim the arrow. Don't grip the **riser** too tightly or in a rigid manner. Try to relax as much as possible without slumping.

A proper stance is important in getting the shot.

Very young archers just starting out with the sport would do well to frequently practice their archer's stance to gain experience and develop their personal technique. More experienced archers should also practice frequently as well to make sure they are always in top form.

DID YOU KNOW?

Howard Hill was a famous American archer from Wilsonville, Alabama. Hill became very famous on and off of movie sets for his skill with a bow and arrow. An extremely accomplished big game hunter, Hill once killed a large elephant armed with nothing but a bow and extra long arrows. Hill not only set records for the longest flight shot, but he also won 196 consecutive archery competitions. In 1975, his name was posthumously entered into the Bowhunters Hall of Fame for his outstanding achievements as one of the greatest hunters of his era.

Well known in Hollywood during the 1930's and 1940's, Hill produced films and lent his technical expertise to other movies. He enjoyed doing amazing tricks with his bow, sometimes shooting a piece of fruit off another person's head or a coin out of the air, all from a seemingly impossible distance. He would also perform trick shots using his feet rather than his hands.

TEXT-DEPENDENT QUESTIONS:

1. Name the four types of bows. How are they different?

2. What procedure should a young hunter use to get into a deer stand with bows and arrows?

3. What is a broadhead arrowhead? How should they be treated differently than other arrowheads?

RESEARCH PROJECT:

Research how hunting wild game helps support our planet's ecosystem by balancing the overpopulation of animals such as deer, rabbits, and squirrels and predators such as coyotes and wolves. List at least four websites to document your findings. Write a two-page report and read it aloud to fellow hunters, family members, and classmates.

Words to Understand:

blind: A simple structure built in the wild that allows hunters to stay hidden from their prey.

hypothermia: A dangerous medical condition when a person's body can't retain heat and stay warm.

CHAPTER 4
OTHER EQUIPMENT

CHOOSING HUNTING CLOTHING

In autumn, the days are cooler but not yet cold. Young hunters in the southern part of America will need lighter weight clothing than hunters that live further north and in Canada. Choose your hunting clothing in shades of tan and brown for solid colors and camouflage for patterned clothing. For cooler temperatures for an early morning hunt, try layering your clothing for more warmth when it's needed. When the temperature begins to rise later in the day, you can easily remove the extra layers for more comfort.

Proper clothing does make a difference in whether or not you enjoy your hunting trip.

A young hunter needs as much physical comfort as possible when hunting because any distraction can break their concentration and cause an accident. Don't let clothing become a problem! Make sure it's not too tight, too short, or too long, so it will function properly and be an asset instead of a liability.

Don't just buy clothing without trying it on first. "Try before you buy" and make sure everything fits well. By using some planning, you can make sure you are comfortably clothed and ready to concentrate on the hunt.

A young hunter that focuses on not tripping because of pants that are too long, or trying to move silently through brush in a too big, floppy hunting jacket won't have the best of luck in bagging game. Some prey, such as wild turkeys, are extremely alert and observant, and the hunter needs to move as silently as possible to get close enough to fire on them.

Be sure to check with state or province regulations and make sure all hunting outfits include the right amount of blaze orange colored items. Hunters need to wear blaze orange to alert other hunters of their presence in the wild. You should never hunt without wearing at least one article of clothing in blaze orange.

HUNTING NEAR WATER

Hunting near water or in swamps or marshlands calls for waterproof clothing and boots, usually wading boots or waders. When duck hunting, you may occasionally need to wade through the water to place duck decoys, and it pays to be prepared with appropriate waterproof footwear. No young hunter should risk exposure to cold water in freezing temperatures. Wearing wet clothing in cold weather can cause **hypothermia**. Make sure that all the clothing you wear in very cold weather is kept warm and dry.

WADERS FOR DRY FEET

Waders are pants with rubber boots attached to the bottom and straps that go over the shoulders to hold them secure on the young hunter's body. Using waders while hunting in swamps or marshlands will protect feet from moisture, sharp sticks, thorns, or rocks encountered in swamps.

Wearing the right foot gear around water will keep you warm and comfortable so you can focus on hunting rather than on staying warm.

BEWARE THE SNAKE

Another danger when hunting in swamps or marshlands that deserves particular mention concerns poisonous snakes. In the southern part of the United States, the snakes most often encountered are usually the aggressive cottonmouth, or water moccasin, as it is sometimes known. In the northern part of the United States and Canada, look out for the eastern massasauga rattlesnake. When buying waders or other rubber boots for hunting in wet areas, be sure to check if the footwear is snake-proof as well as waterproof. Wearing snake-proof boots could save your life.

When entering a blind for the first time, be sure to look for snakes. Reptiles like to hide in dark and hidden places, so let an adult check out the interior first.

In another part of the United States, rattlesnakes can pose a significant problem for all ages of hunters. When hunting in areas where these venomous snakes are a problem, be sure to wear snake-proof boots to protect your feet and legs from the possibility of a snakebite. Always carry a snakebite kit with your gear.

Watch out for snakes and other dangers in the woods.

WATCH OUT FOR ALLIGATORS

When hunting in swamps in the southern part of the United States, watch out for alligators! Alligators are usually lethargic by the time autumn rolls around, but you can never be too careful when dealing with these dangerous reptiles. When an alligator lies motionless in the water, they resemble a log and can be hard to identify. A young hunter should never hunt without an experienced adult in alligator-infested swamps or lakes.

Hunters have been attacked and bitten by alligators when duck hunting near bodies of water. These massive and super-strong reptiles have big mouths full of very sharp teeth that can slice flesh and powerful jaws that can break bones.

Alligators have been known to bite hunters who invade their territory.

HUNTING JACKETS

Hunting jackets are heavily insulated and constructed from a super-tough material that will withstand tears and rips from bushes, briars, and twigs. If you choose a jacket that comes with a zip-out liner, you can remove it when the sun shines too hot. Young hunters need a jacket that isn't too tight to restrict movement but also not so loose as to cause a distraction while hunting. Jackets that are too big and bulky can pose a problem when bowhunting because the jacket can obstruct the bowstring.

Hunting clothing designed for wet areas have a distinct camouflage print that blends well with the surrounding landscape. You can also buy hunting clothing in a multitude of camo prints to match the hunting terrain. There is camo for snowy areas, wooded areas, or desert terrain.

Make sure to buy hunting jackets that are right for the surroundings.

USE PROPER GLOVES

When hunting in winter, a young hunter needs to be able to stay warm and comfortable for extended periods of time. It's really difficult to shoot a bow or pull the trigger of a shotgun with half-frozen fingers. You will need to protect your fingers from the cold and wind if you want to be able to have a successful hunt.

When buying gloves, make sure they aren't too large as to make the handling of a weapon difficult. Insulated gloves will help keep hands warm in winter cold and prevent clumsy fumbling with a firearm and missed targets. Some gloves feature a mitten-like covering that fits over the glove for an extra layer of protection from the freezing cold. Other types of mittens fold back to expose the bare fingers and can be used when the weather is warmer.

The right glove can keep you warm and aid your hunting.

You will need to experiment with different glove sizes to find out which one fits you best. Glove sizes vary with different manufacturers, so remember to try before you buy. Never assume a glove will fit just because your size is on the label.

Some gloves come equipped with a special lining to help prevent body heat from escaping. These gloves hold the heat inside the glove to keep hands warm and supple for shooting. Some hunting clothing also offers the option of masking a hunter's scent so animals, such as deer, won't know there are humans in the area.

HUNTING BOOTS

Boots should fit a young hunter's feet well. Boots that are too loose can cause blisters when walking long distances, and the pain can be a dangerous distraction. It's hard to concentrate on gun safety when your blistered feet are hurting badly, and all you want to do is sit down and take them off.

Hunting boots are designed to help a hunter walk longer and more comfortably, but it's important to get the right size for your feet. Remember to try before you buy. Don't let someone else, like a parent, buy the boots before you can try them on first. You need to find out how the boots fit before buying them.

Wearing thick socks with your boots can provide another layer of protection against blisters on long hikes. Insulated boots will keep feet warmer in cold weather, and waterproof boots will keep socks and feet dry.

The right boot means the difference between comfortable or miserable feet.

HUNTING VESTS

These vests have all sorts of special pockets and compartments to store ammo and gear. If you wear a hunting vest under a jacket, this can provide an extra layer for warmth in very cold weather. Some vests are designed for a specific type of hunting, such as turkey hunting. A turkey hunting vest has pouches to hold turkey calls or decoys, ammo, and water containers.

Whitetail Deer Hunting Gear.

DEER STANDS

Sometimes called a tree stand, these enclosed or open platforms are built on tall posts to allow a hunter to spot deer or other game approaching from a far distance. Some deer stands are built around existing trees to add stability to the structure, and some are enclosed with a roof, walls, and open spaces for observation.

The best season to use a deer stand is in the fall and winter when the leaves have fallen from the trees. Naked tree limbs provide the best visibility. Observation from a deer stand can help you track the movements of wild game and choose which animal you want to shoot.

Using a body harness while in a deer stand can prevent accidental falls, especially if you go to sleep in the stand waiting for that elusive deer. Snap the harness on immediately after entering the deer stand and don't take it off until you are ready to leave.

Deer stands provide great views of approaching deer.

SAFETY FIRST!

Don't carry a firearm or bows and arrows up into a deer stand. Young hunters should climb into the deer stand first and then haul up their equipment using a cord, called a hauling line.

Always check the condition of a deer stand for signs of deterioration before climbing up onto the platform. You don't want to step on a rotten ladder rung and fall to the ground. Make sure the rungs can support a person's body weight by stamping on them hard with your foot. Check the stability of the overall structure as well. If the upper platform seems unsafe or unstable, climb down immediately.

Remember to check carefully for any stinging insects that may have made a nest within the structure, especially in the early fall before the frosts and cold have killed them. Some insects, such as wasps or yellow jackets, can attack in a swarm, so be alert to the possibility of their presence. You don't want to be stung multiple times. If you have an allergy to insect venom, be sure to carry the appropriate treatment in your backpack. You may be many miles from a medical treatment facility when on a hunt.

Bringing a cell phone on a hunt for phone access in case of emergency is a good idea. Turn off the ringer and store the phone inside a waterproof bag in a backpack.

Make sure the deer stand is safe before climbing in.

A DRY CHANGE OF CLOTHING

When planning a hunt in wet areas such as swamps or marshland during very cold weather, be sure to pack a change of clothing. Wearing wet clothing in cold weather can cause hypothermia, which can be a dangerous medical condition.

Roll a spare pair of pants into a tight cylinder and secure with large rubber bands. The pants will not take up a lot of room in a backpack this way. Pack a spare pair of dry socks as well.

After removing wet pants, roll them tightly and secure with large rubber bands. Place the wet garment in a waterproof bag and store in a backpack.

Having the right hunting equipment on a hunt is extremely important.

BLINDS

Blinds are different from deer stands because they are located on the ground instead of raised in the air. Blinds are typically rustic wooden structures that allow hunters to observe wild game without being seen. The structure can also be covered with tree limbs and dead leaves for camouflage.

Some hunters heat their blinds in freezing weather with portable propane heaters. However, never attempt to do this on your own. An adult should always be present to check the fuel supply, light the heater, make sure there is enough ventilation, and extinguish the heater after use. Only heaters approved for indoor use should be used in a hunting blind. You don't want to risk the possibility of carbon monoxide poisoning.

Like a deer stand, check out the blind for stinging insects that may have made a nest inside and also for snakes that may have entered the structure. Animals, such as rats, skunks, and opossums, can also inhabit a hunting blind if it's been empty for a time.

Before entering the blind for the first time, make a lot of noise to scare away any animals. Bang on the outside with a stick or rock for a minute or two to give any animal inside a chance to run away. You don't want to enter the blind and try to force an animal out. They may try to bite.

A good hunting blind will camouflage your hunting party.

KAYAKS OR BOATS

Boats or kayaks are sometimes used for duck or geese hunting when searching lakes or rivers for the waterfowls. Young hunters should never travel in a boat or kayak without a life jacket. These life-saving devices are available in camouflage colors that will also help disguise hunters while hunting.

Don't wear waders or heavy rubber boots when traveling in boats. If the boat capsizes, you need to be able to swim to land, and these types of heavy rubber boots will make it very difficult to do so.

When boarding a boat, make sure to take the ammo out of all of the guns. Store the guns and ammunition safely, as well as bows and arrows. Never bring a loaded gun into a boat because it could misfire and blow a hole in the bottom of the boat, causing it to sink. Don't overload a boat with too many people or hunting gear. An overloaded boat can tip and overturn very easily.

If it starts to rain, don't linger on the lake or stream. Hunters should head for the shore as quickly as possible. Don't sit in a boat during a storm because of the danger of lightning strikes. Heavy rain or rough water can also swamp the boat and cause it to sink.

Hunting water fowl from a boat can prove successful.

FOOD AND DRINK WHILE HUNTING

When eating on a hunt, remember to be silent! Avoid any noisy food wrappers such as crinkly plastic or foil. Crunchy foods such as potato chips, popcorn, or roasted nuts can also make enough sound that will alert deer or other prey that a human is lurking nearby. Any food that is juicy or in half liquid form, such as soup, probably isn't a good idea to take on a hunt because it would be difficult to eat.

Foods that contain a lot of sugar aren't a good choice either because sugar can make you hyper. A hunter needs to remain observant and be calm in order not to make mistakes. Hunting in the woods is not the time to be hyperactive because of an overload of sugar. Sugar also gets processed by the body very quickly, shooting up blood sugar then dropping energy levels and causing fatigue. So not only will you feel hyperactive at first, but you will feel tired and sluggish afterward, causing you to make mistakes.

Solid, nutritious food provides the energy a young hunter needs to remain vigilant and energetic. Choose ready-to-eat foods that can be stored in a backpack and are easily opened and eaten, preferably without the use of utensils.

Choose snacks that are high in nutrition, low in sugar, and provide energy.

Hiking through woods or fields can give a young hunter a healthy appetite. Before leaving on a hunt, you should always eat a good meal to ensure hunger will not strike again for several hours. This situation can be especially true for younger hunters. When hungry, you tend to become more careless which can be dangerous when handling weapons.

Water is the best drink to take on a hunting trip. Water hydrates the body for quicker reflexes and lubricates the eyes for sharper vision. Water bottles create unnecessary litter and can be easily punctured and leak. Transport water in a canteen like soldiers use.

DID YOU KNOW?

President Theodore Roosevelt was one of the world's most famous hunters that enjoyed camping and spending time in the wilderness. When Roosevelt was on a hunting trip in Mississippi in 1902, a black bear was captured, and the president decided to spare the animal's life. The result of that incident was the invention of the Teddy Bear. Roosevelt also worked to establish National Parks in the United States to preserve large expanses of pristine wilderness for future generations.

President Theodore Roosevelt enjoyed the outdoors, including hunting.

TEXT-DEPENDENT QUESTIONS:

1. What do hunters typically use to camouflage a blind?

2. Why should a young hunter avoid wet clothing on a cold winter day?

3. Why should sugar not be eaten on a long hunt?

RESEARCH PROJECT:

Compare the way ammunition for a rifle works with that of shotgun ammo. How do they work differently? What are the pros and cons of each? Get opinions from three adult hunters and compare them. Write down your thoughts on which ammunitions would work the best in different situations and with different types of wild game. Discuss your thoughts with the three adult hunters and write down their responses. How did their opinions differ from yours?

SERIES GLOSSARY OF KEY TERMS

Briars: A patch of thick underbrush that is full of thorny bushes. Rabbits and other small game love to hide in these.

Burrow: A hole made by a small animal where they live and stay safe from predators. It is also the word for what an animal does when it digs these holes.

Carcass: The dead body of an animal after the innards have been removed and before it has been skinned.

Field dress: To remove the inner organs from an animal after it has been harvested. It's important to field dress an animal as quickly as possible after it has been harvested.

Habitat: The area in which an animal lives. It's important to preserve animal habitats.

Hide: The skin of an animal once it has been removed from the animal. Hides can be made into clothing and other useful gear.

Homestead: A place or plot of land where a family makes their home. This is different from habitat because it is manmade.

Kmph: An abbreviation for kilometers per hour, which is a metric unit of measurement for speed. One kilometer is equal to approximately .62 miles.

Marsh: A wet area of land covered with grasses. The water in a marsh is often hidden by cattail, grasses, and other plants.

Maul: To attack and injure—either an animal or human being can be mauled.

Mph: An abbreviation for miles per hour, which is a unit of measurement for speed. One mile is equal to approximately 1.61 kilometers.

Pepper spray: A chemical used to repel bears and other dangerous creatures. It causes irritation and burning to the skin and eyes.

Poaching: The act of harvesting an animal at a time and place where it is illegal. Always follow the local hunting laws and regulations.

Process a kill: This is when an animal is butchered and cut up into pieces of meat to prepare for cooking. A kill can be processed by yourself or commercially.

Prey: Animals that are hunted for food—either by humans or other animals. It can also mean the act of hunting.

Roosting: What birds do when they rest upon a branch or a tree. Roosting keeps sleeping birds safe from predators.

Scout: To look ahead and observe an area. It is important to scout an area before hunting there. It helps you find evidence of your prey.

Suburbia: The area, people, and culture of a suburban, which is an area outside of a city or town where people live. It is often a small area full of houses.

Swamp: An area of wet land covered in grasses, trees, and other plant life. A swamp is not a good place to build a home, but it can be a good place to hunt.

Thicket: A collection of bushes and branches where small animals, like rabbits and rodents, like to hide.

Timid: A lack of confidence; shy. Rabbits, deer, and birds are often timid, which helps keep them alert and safe from predators.

Vegetation: All of the plant life in an area.

INDEX

FURTHER READING

Thompson, David R. *Young Hunter: Stories for Beginning Hunters and Their Mentors*. Indianapolis: Dog Ear Publishing, 2014.

Waguespack, Michael. *The Deer Hunting Book: Short Stories for Young Hunters*. Kansas City: Country Kid Publishing LLC, 2013.

Waguespack, Michael. *My First Deer Hunt*. Kansas City: Country Kid Publishing LLC, 2015

Chandler, Matt. *Deer Hunting for Kids (Into the Great Outdoors)*. North Mankato: Capstone Press, 2013.

INTERNET RESOURCES

https://youtu.be/jLLnGM3DXE0
Shellhaas, Dave. Outdoor Kids Club Ultimate Hunting Guide. Miami: Miami Valley Outdoor Media, Limited, 2011.

https://youtu.be/IvBWCCsHhDY
What is Shotgun Fit? - Sporting Clays Tip. The National Shooting Sports Foundation. YouTube, 2011.

https://youtu.be/PHbEXJGZBEA
When You Don't Know What to Do - Sporting Clays Tip. The National Shooting Sports Foundation. YouTube, 2014.

https://youtu.be/XvgyI-Zyf-U
Deer Hunting with a Bow: Introduction. Field to Feast. YouTube, 2013.

https://youtu.be/ahLNCzV56yk
Beginning Archery 101 - What You Need to Know - with Renowned Coach John Dudley. Nockonarchery. YouTube, 2017.

https://youtu.be/V47OptEK6F0
Archery Tips - 10 Things Beginners Do (And Why You Shouldn't). NUSensi. YouTube, 2017.

https://youtu.be/dbbevyob1zg
Choosing Camo for Deer Hunting. Yamaha Whitetail Diaries. YouTube, 2011.

https://youtu.be/dPYOBYkktJA
Montana Rifle Elk Hunting - Basic Gear for a Day Hunt. Randy Newberg, Hunter. YouTube, 2016

ORGANIZATIONS TO CONTACT

The National Shooting Sports Foundation
Flintlock Ridge Office Center
11 Mile Hill Road
Newton, CT 06470-2359
Phone: (203) 426-1320
Fax: (203) 426-1087
Internet: https://www.nssf.org/

National Firearms Association
P.O. Box 49090
Edmonton, Alberta
Canada T6E 6H4
Phone: 1-877-818-0393
Fax: 780-439-4091
Internet: https://www.nfa.ca

The International Hunter Education Association
800 East 73rd Ave, Unit 2
Denver, CO 80229
Phone: 303-430-7233
Fax: 303-430-7236
Internet: https://www.ihea-usa.org

The National Wildlife Federation
11100 Wildlife Center Drive
Reston, VA 20190
Phone: 1-800-822-9919
Internet: https://www.nwf.org

PHOTO CREDITS

VIDEO CREDITS

Chapter 1
How Wildlife is Thriving Because of Guns and Hunting: http://x-qr.net/1G6o

Chapter 2
Cowboy Shotgunning Equipment and Loading - Cowboy Action Shooting: http://x-qr.net/1DCn

Chapter 3
Proper Release and Bow Hand Placement for Archery: http://x-qr.net/1Goh.

Chapter 4
Whitetail Deer Hunting Gear: http://x-qr.net/1Hmr

AUTHOR'S BIOGRAPHY

Elizabeth Dee has hunted extensively in the southeast part of the United States for small and large game. She has also cleaned and cooked game for family meals. Elizabeth has been writing for over 25 years for magazines and web articles.